On God's Train

On God's Train

FRANCIS POLE

StoryTerrace

CONTENTS

1. EARLY LIFE (1942-1948)

When we were small, my sister Veronica and I spent a lot of time playing under tables.

I am sure this must date from the war years, before Veronica was even born, when I grew used to playing in our family's indoor Morrison shelter, which was rather like a cage but with a solid top. One day when I was three years old, I was under a desk in the so-called nursery of our home in Gillingham when my father came in and gave me a wooden toy train with five trucks, each with red wheels. I remember this as if it were yesterday. I loved trains! My mother – though more often Auntie Dorothy, the babysitter – used to take me in my pushchair to a level crossing to watch the steam trains go by. Later, I became the proud owner of a clockwork Hornby train set, which Veronica and I spent hours playing with on my bedroom floor. Later still, when working in The Hague, I bought some (electric) 'N' gauge Fleischmann track and trains, comprised of German, Dutch and Swiss engines and coaches.

My parents, Kary and Magda (short for Magdalene) Pollaczek, were born in Vienna in 1902 and 1909 respectively. My father came from a family of non-practising Jews, and my mother, too, was of Jewish stock but brought up a Lutheran. They both converted to Catholicism early in their marriage. My father's own parents had an unhappy marriage, which ended with my grandfather's suicide when my father was 11. I have faint memories of my grandmother looking very severe and always wearing black. She lived for a while in a convent in north London, before returning to Vienna, where she died in 1950.

My mother's father, Egon Wellesz, was a musicologist and composer of some renown, and a professor of Byzantine music at Vienna University. He was in Holland, where a large work of his, *Prosperos Beschwörungen*, was being performed, when Germany invaded Austria in March 1938. He fled to Oxford – where he already had connections with Lincoln College – and settled there for the rest of his life. His wife Emmy, my grandmother, was a doctor of Persian art, who could speak six languages fluently. She returned to Vienna after my grandfather's death and carried on teaching in her rooms until the age of 96. She was a formidable person, but deep down a lovely woman.

My mother was a schoolgirl when she first met my medical student father, who was seven years her senior. She had just turned 18 and passed her matriculation – and my father his Doctor of Medicine examinations – when they married in 1927. My father promptly sent her for cookery lessons. In time she became a good pastry cook, but to begin with, she'd often order the food for the meal she had learned to cook the previous day, thus hiding from their maid her lack of expertise!

After Hitler's invasion of Austria, my father quickly realised the threat to his family's safety. By now an eminent pathologist, he, my mother and my sister Gabriele – who had been born in 1934 – escaped to my mother's cousins in Switzerland. Almost overnight, they had gone from being a prosperous family to homeless refugees. Thanks to connections of my grandfather in Oxford, my father received help to obtain a study visa, which allowed him to come to Britain and re-qualify as a doctor. He arrived in Dover in October 1938, with my mother and Gabriele following a few weeks later.

After sitting his medical examinations again, this time in Edinburgh, my father found a job as junior partner to a GP, a New Zealander called Norman Porterfield, in Gillingham, Kent, and the family moved into a bungalow in Pump Lane. But in 1940, as an 'enemy alien', he was interned on the Isle of Man for three months. This experience proved to be more pleasant than it might have been as he was elected 'house father' and was clearly respected by the other interns, enjoying his responsibilities – which included being everyone's counsellor.

Thanks to pressure from friends, he was released, and in October 1940 the family were together again in Kent. As Dr Porterfield had joined the forces, my father looked after the practice by himself for most of the war years. Three days after their move to a house with a purpose-built surgery on South Avenue, Gillingham, three incendiary bombs landed on my parents' previous home – in the very spots where they sat every evening in their armchairs.

I was born at 25 South Avenue on 17th February 1942.

I do have some memories of the war years. Chatham Dockyard was nearby and we lived opposite the Gordon Barracks, a base of the Royal Engineers, so were subject to regular air raids. I remember Lancaster bombers passing overhead for what seemed a long time after the war. We had an air raid shelter in the garden as well as the Morrison shelter, but I remember it more as a playhouse for Veronica (born in 1945) and me – while my mother used it to store jam and stewed fruit.

Despite his strong Austrian accent, my father became a Major in the Home Guard and was appointed medical officer to a station eight miles away at Hoo. It was a dangerous journey to make in the dark, with the car headlights masked.

When I was older, I sometimes accompanied him on his home visits, standing on the green leather passenger seat of his car – registration AJH 46 – my head sticking out of the open roof, as he drove through the Kent countryside. Some of the farmers used to give us eggs or fruit, which was wonderful, as food was still rationed.

My grandparents, whom we called Pupapa and Mumama, visited us two or three times a year in the school holidays. Veronica and I were always keen to help them unpack because we knew there would be a present for us in their luggage! Apart from spending time in the garden, especially during the summer, we used to play 'houses' with them in nearby woods.

My grandfather never really got over the war. He listened to the news every day, and if there was the slightest hint of trouble in the world he'd become quite anxious. He, too, had been interned on the Isle of Man, but in his case it had almost led to a nervous breakdown.

When I was about four and a half I started kindergarten at St Joseph's Convent in Chatham. Every morning my father took me to catch the brown and cream bus at Rainham Mark, entrusting me to some older pupil. One morning, one of the wheels of our rather old bus came off and went running down Chatham Hill! At kindergarten I remember writing on slates, learning to count, and singing. My father was doctor to the convent, and sometimes we would be invited to tea. On my sixth birthday the nuns made a cake for me. I was expected to sing for everyone, and the nuns clapped enthusiastically. It was all very embarrassing!

Seven years my senior, Gabriele doesn't feature as much as Veronica in my childhood memories. By the time I was born she was already boarding with the nuns of Notre Dame in Devon, and while I was still at prep school, left home to start her nurse's training. But Veronica and I had adventures on our bikes, and enjoyed spending our pocket money on sweets in the corner shop. I do remember, though, when we were all at home together in the holidays, how Gabriele used to cheat at Monopoly. As the oldest, she was always the banker, and if she was losing she would suddenly decide to dish out more money to us all!

In September 1948, when I was six and a half, I was packed off to St Augustine's Abbey School in Huntingdonshire. Veronica would join Gabriele in Teignmouth, but later transferred to Les Oiseaux, a convent boarding school in Westgate-on-Sea, much nearer home. One of the main reasons my parents sent us all to boarding school was so that we would grow up without the pronounced Austrian accents that they naturally both still had.

It was my starting at prep school that led to the changing of our family surname by deed poll after my future headmaster said to my father that Pollaczek was not going to be an easy name for the school to deal with. So my father shortened it to

Pole, a good Catholic name. I once considered changing it back to Pollaczek, but my father, who had become a British citizen in 1947, was dead against it. In a way, I think that he was happy to shrug off his Austrian background, though keeping the bits he wanted.

In readiness for my new school, a whole new outfit was required, which meant a trip to Harrods of Knightsbridge. While my parents were otherwise occupied, I became bored, and wandered off to a nearby escalator, going up to the next floor where I assumed that the down escalator I could see would take me back to where I'd started. Of course it didn't. I tried another up escalator, assuming I would get back to where I had been before, but again, I was wrong! Eventually, feeling very lost, I spoke to a member of staff, who took me to the lost property office where the very nice man in charge announced over the tannoy that he had a little boy of six, awaiting collection.

My parents were not impressed, although later it gave them something to talk about to their friends.

WAPPEN AUS DEM GESCHLECHTE

The family crest of Loeb, my father's mother's family

Our 3 children in 1947.

living conditions he could

Gabriele, Veronica and me in 1947

My parents, sisters and me in 1956

My maternal grandparents, Egon and Emmy Wellesz, with my nieces Michelle and Philippa

2. SCHOOLDAYS (1948-1959)

I was understandably fairly nervous to be leaving home for the first time, and at such a young age, to start my new school. St Augustine's Abbey School was in the village of Hemingford Grey, which today lies in Cambridgeshire. The journey began by catching the 4.10 p.m. train to Huntingdon from platform six at King's Cross Station in specially reserved coaches. Today it takes 40 minutes, but our slow train rattled along for two hours.

My trunk, which had been collected from home thanks to the railway's Luggage in Advance service, was waiting for me at the junior dormitory in St John's, a rather forbidding three-storey house about a quarter of a mile from the rest of the school. It was sparely furnished: the beds were basic and the lightbulbs had no shades. The headmaster, Father Edward, and the other three monks had been in the armed services, and the school was run on almost military lines.

The day began early with chapel for Mass, followed by breakfast, and then 'parade' in the grounds at 8.10 a.m., when we were inspected by Father Edward to ensure that we had washed our faces, behind our ears and our knees. Only boys over five feet tall were allowed to wear long trousers. Parade happened every morning, regardless of the weather, after which we had playtime. Although not allowed indoors, several of us did sneak inside to play on cold winter days and, when we heard adult footsteps on the stairs, jumped out of the first-floor window. The first lesson began at nine o'clock.

It was only three years since the war had ended, and food was still rationed. Lunch, the main meal, might be stew – a couple of bits of meat and lots of gravy – or herrings or kippers, which were bony as hell! If there was something we really didn't like, we would surreptitiously slide one of the leaves of the table, pop the food into a cavity, and creep back later to dispose of it. This ruse was discovered eventually – probably because of the smell! The monks, who ate in a room next door to us, had far better food than we did.

After lunch, sport was the main activity – something at which I was pretty useless. Some of us who weren't sporty enjoyed Cubs and Scouts instead. A meagre tea was soon followed by supper, during which we sat in silence while one of the boys read to us from the Rule of St Benedict and from a book that Father Edward had chosen. There was a short playtime before bed.

Both the classroom block and the main house were very cold, and often there was ice not only outside the windows but on the inside too, especially in the dormitories.

Punishments were severe, and if a boy did not own up to something which affected us all, either we were all caned or we suffered a 'blitz' detention, in which we had to sit silently and perfectly still at our desks for an hour.

Father Edward used a bamboo cane and was fairly accurate in his delivery, but Father Norbert, the deputy headmaster, was as blind as a bat and his beatings often landed halfway up our backs or round our knees!

My first teacher was Miss Atkinson, the only woman teacher, who was strict but very fair. When she was cross about something, she would thump us on the back. Mr Avico, another lay teacher, was very strict too. When some bright spark let off a stink bomb on a hot summer day, he closed all the windows of the classroom, saying that if he could put up with the smell, so could we!

Halfway through the term my parents came to visit. They usually drove up on the Saturday and took me out for lunch. I would see them again briefly on the Sunday morning before they left for home. Generally, I enjoyed these visits, although occasionally I rather wished that they hadn't come because the meeting only exacerbated feelings of homesickness.

As I got older, I was regularly chosen to read during the evening meal, which meant that afterwards I ate the better food left over by the monks. Because I had been at the school for so long, I gradually became headmaster's 'pet', which led to some privileges and duties, one of which was film projectionist at our weekly film night. I suspect that the films were more for the monks' entertainment than ours: a showing of *Dr Jekyll and Mr Hyde* – with an H (horror) certificate – had several of us terrified for days after!

The school was haunted. I saw the ghost one night, when I was about 12 years old. We were all in bed when a whitish shape drifted through an open doorway from dormitory seven, floated through my dormitory (number eight) and carried on through the closed door that led to dormitory nine. No one was scared. It was more a case of, 'Did you see that?!' We believe it may have been the ghost of a monk who had been buried in the grounds. Many years later, when visiting what had been the classroom block – now turned into two flats – a friend and I were asked not to mention the ghost to the children. Apparently, it was still around.

Tragically, during my first year at the school, a friend and one of the monks both died from drowning in the Great Ouse – the latter whilst saving a boy from drowning – while the following year a friend's brother died in a polio outbreak. Despite all this, I look back on my seven years at Hemingford Grey as a happy time.

I was less happy at Downside, in Somerset, which I began in September 1955. Perhaps things would have been different if my asthma hadn't been so bad – this was before inhalers were invented. I remember hearing the doctor say to matron, 'That was close,' as I was coming round after one particularly serious attack. But by forging both the doctor's and my housemaster's signatures, I got out of games. While the others were on the playing fields, my friend Paul and I worked in the kitchen stores, where we stuffed ourselves with biscuits!

In Junior House my housemaster was Father Brendan, an eccentric Irishman. He would invite some of us to his room in the evening, where we would cook toast on his electric fire. In senior house I had Dom Aelred Watkin. He found any opportunity he could to cane me, and seemed to particularly relish doing so.

The headmaster, Dom Wilfred Passmore, administered his punishments with a whalebone bound in leather, called a tolly. You either had your trousers up or down, depending on his mood. He was a great character, and I liked and respected him enormously.

I didn't excel academically at Downside, which had a reputation as a Catholic crammer. I sat 'O' levels at 15 and 'A' levels in French and Spanish a year later. After getting 'O' level passes, I stayed on another year to re-sit them – and got the same results. I am sure I would have done better in Classics or science but had been given no choice in the matter.

Every summer my parents took part in a Catholic conference in Ramsgate. That was where I met my first girlfriend, Liz. Her mother, in particular, thought that I was the best thing since sliced bread! I can't remember how our relationship ended. It was probably because of the distance between her home in Reading and mine in Gillingham.

Downside Abbey and School

Downside schoolboy: me in 1957

3. RAILWAY AND SEMINARY
(1959-1968)

I had disappointed my parents and my grandfather in not achieving the grades to go up to Oxford. In fact, my parents were so perturbed by my lack of academic prowess that they took me to cousin Josefine, a child psychiatrist and friend of the psychoanalyst Anna Freud, who, happily, pronounced me quite normal! The one saving grace was that my siblings did not go to university either. Gabriele had joined the RAF after training as a nurse at Westminster Hospital, while Veronica did a Pitman secretarial course when she finished school.

After leaving Downside in 1959, I had an appointment with the Public Schools Appointments Bureau, and told them that I was interested in railways. An interview was organised for me with the Assistant General Manager of Southern Region and the Chief Staff Officer. I think they were surprised to find a 17-year-old public schoolboy sitting before them.

'What do you think about the new diesels coming in to replace steam?' one of them asked me.

I was confident in my reply. 'To be honest, I think it's a big mistake.'

'Why do you say that?'

'Well, we've just had the Suez crisis, and the supply of oil was interrupted. What is going to happen with the diesel if we have another incident like that? I think they ought to extend electrification.'

There was a pause, before they said, 'Personally we agree with you.'

They offered me a Traffic Apprenticeship. This was a new scheme for accelerated promotion. 'To start with, we're going to send you as a booking clerk to a station called Snodland in Kent.'

The only problem was the anti-social hours. The office opened at 5.20 a.m., which meant I had to get up at 3.15 a.m., catch a train at 4 from Gillingham to Strood, then get the paper train from Strood to Maidstone West and alight at Snodland. After a while, the senior clerk told me I could start coming in a bit later. All the same, I took the view that, if I was to manage people in the future, I needed to familiarise myself with every job going, so sometimes I used to sleep on the first-aid stretcher in the booking office, next to the coal fire, and after just a few hours' sleep, head for the shunting yards. There was a cement factory just up the road where shunting carried on until around two in the morning. I watched them at work and they even let me drive a shunter.

I really saw the railways as my career.

One of my jobs was to do the books which recorded the income from the sale of the different types of tickets. The vertical and horizontal columns both had to agree, but mine never did. One day the auditor came to inspect them – and announced that they were the worst books he'd ever seen!

After a month at Halling, the next station to Snodland, I moved to Dr Beeching's office at Oxford Circus (though I never met the man himself), where I worked with Peter Reeve, the son of the then Bishop of Lichfield. Sometimes we had to go to Southampton to collect computer tapes and bring them back for analysis. On more than one occasion, the ticket inspector would pounce into the first-class car, clearly not expecting a couple of 18-year-olds to be sitting there. His manner would change when we showed him our first-class passes. 'Thank you very much' he would reply deferentially.

In the rolling stock department at Waterloo, my boss, Mr Orme, didn't like public schoolboys. I didn't think much of him either. When a job in the Shipping and Continental department caught my eye, he thought my application premature as it was a grade above my own, and refused to recommend me.

To his — and my own — surprise, I got the job.

At 19, I was the youngest person on the railway to reach grade three — and with it, the princely annual salary of £655. My first pay packet had been two pounds 17 shillings and five pence — so I felt like a millionaire!

The Shipping and Continental department was based in offices above the forecourt near platform two at Victoria Station. My job was to record the punctuality of the cross-Channel ferries and follow up any delays. I had some interesting colleagues there. Mr Boolaki used to tell me he didn't want to go to heaven as he'd get bored praying. Another had been a judge at the Nuremberg trials, while the secretary I shared went berserk — cursing and swearing — whenever there was a full moon. A genuine lunatic!

In my lunch hour I often visited Westminster Cathedral, where one day I spotted a leaflet. It had a picture of a boy on the front, and its title was, 'Do you want to be a Priest?' I bought it, along with an encyclical about priesthood, skim-read them on the train home, and left them there. The next time I was in the cathedral they caught my eye again.

We had a lovely parish priest in Gillingham, Father Scott. Sometimes the pair of us had a glass of sherry together. One day he said to me, 'Francis, what do you want to do with your life?'

I blurted out, 'I think I want to be a priest.'

'Funny you should say that because I think you'd be very suitable. I'm seeing the rector of a seminary tomorrow and I'll get the forms.'

Before I knew it I was being called to interview with the Bishop of Southwark, Cyril Cowderoy, who sat surrounded by all his canons. I'd had second thoughts by then, and when the Bishop asked me why I wanted to be a priest, I replied, 'I don't think I do, actually, but I think God is telling me to be.'

This precipitated lots of whispering amongst the canons. But they must have thought me suitable, as in 1962, at the age of 20 – after three years working for the railways – I began my training at St John's Seminary at Wonersh, near Guildford.

I dropped a clanger on my first day there. One of the priests, James McConnon, wanted to know where we'd all been before coming to Wonersh. Most of my fellow seminarians had been to junior seminary at Mark Cross in East Sussex. Thinking I was being amusing, I replied, 'I've come from the wicked world.' That was it: I was labelled a troublemaker. It wasn't a good start to my relationship with Jim McConnon, either. He taught cosmology and would always try to catch me out with difficult questions.

Our training lasted six years, during which we spent two years studying philosophy and four years theology, as well as scripture and canon law for the whole six years.

At the end of our second year we received the rite of tonsure – a snip of hair by the bishop – which marked our progression from layman to cleric. Towards the end of the following two years we were received into what are known as the Minor Orders: Porter, Reader, Exorcist and Acolyte. Each is a step for the seminarian on the journey to priesthood. In our fifth year we were ordained Subdeacon and in the following October, Deacon, the final step towards priesthood. Of the 23 who started with me, only 13 became priests.

But it wasn't always an easy journey. I found it quite depressing at times and had quite a temper.

Once – probably about halfway through my training – I felt suicidal, so I went to see Father Fogarty (known as' Fog'), who was my spiritual director and a man with remarkable insight.

'Come in, come in, I was waiting to see you,' he said warmly.

When I told him I felt depressed, he said, 'It's no good throwing yourself out of a window, you'd just make a nasty mess.'

Incredibly, I had been thinking of doing exactly that, but after my chat with Fog, I felt better almost immediately. I think I just found the whole experience at Wonersh very claustrophobic.

On a more light-hearted note, a woman living nearby complained that if she stood on a chair that she had placed on her dining-room table, she could see us in our pool, swimming in the nude. Rather than questioning her further, the practice got banned.

On holiday after my second year at the seminary I fell in love with Sharon, the sister of good friends of mine. However, her sister Theresa and brother-in-law Colin did their best to ensure that I carried on with my training and put Sharon out of my mind.

Although the rector threatened to throw me out several times as I wasn't conforming, I always got the thumbs-up at the annual review.

In January 1968, as a newly ordained deacon, I was sent to the large parish of St Mary's in Wellesley Road, Croydon.

Lifelong passion: steam trains

A Southern Electric train: my views on electrification helped to secure my first job

St John's Seminary, Wonersh

The seminary chapel at Wonersh

4. FIRST PARISHES (1968-1971)

The church was packed every Sunday. The register recorded 3,009 attending church over all the weekend Masses, many of whom were Irish.

My main memory of St Mary's is of Palm Sunday.

'Don't forget to wave your palms!' I told the children, whom I knew from the church school.

The truly conservative parish priest reprimanded me for this, which I thought was strange, considering the Gospel accounts of Jesus's entry into Jerusalem.

I didn't get on with my parents' priest, Father Gleeson, who told the Bishop – untruthfully – that I didn't go to church in seminary holidays. (He knew that I went to the neighbouring church.) So, in July 1968, when the time came for my ordination to the priesthood, I accepted an invitation from parish priest Father Trant McCarthy to be ordained in his brand new church in Strood.

My first appointment was to Deptford, where, on the day I arrived, the Irish parish priest informed me that he was about to go on holiday.

'I'd like you to be in charge of the liturgy,' he said. 'Oh, and I've been thinking – we ought to do a census of the parish and see how many people are Catholics.' It really was a case of being thrown in at the deep end.

I became friendly with David, one of our senior servers, a schoolboy in his mid-teens. I appointed him parish Master of

Ceremonies. Together we trailed round all the tower blocks in our parish, knocking on the doors of flats, and asking the residents if they were Catholic. Most people were friendly and happy to engage with us.

David and I have remained friends to this day. He got married to Jill, and became Chief Inspector of the police in Jersey, where I went to stay with him twice – once alone, another time with Nicky and the girls.

Things took a turn for the worse when the parish priest returned from his holiday after six weeks. I used to hear him in his room in the presbytery, below mine, putting the Sunday collection on the horses, swearing away and behaving very uncouthly.

I don't think he thought much of me either. He told me I was too slow saying Mass. His Mass on a weekday took 11 minutes, whereas mine took 23.

He was also suspicious about why I had such a long queue outside my confessional every Saturday. The senior curate also had a long queue, but everyone knew that was because he was very deaf; he would have been less happy about the reason for mine. That summer of 1968, Pope Paul VI had written the encyclical, *Humanae Vitae*, in which he reaffirmed his opposition to artificial contraception.

People would confess to me that they used birth control.

'Is there any particular reason?' I would ask them.

'Well, I live in a tenement flat, I've got six children already, we have to pump up water into the bath . . .'

I'd say, 'I'll give you absolution today, but don't come back.'

'Oh, but the Pope says . . .'

'Don't worry about the Pope. You've got to follow your conscience.'

When the parish priest asked me why my box was so popular, I replied, 'I'm giving Green Shield stamps.'

I grew to love the people of Deptford, which had a large Irish population. On Sundays, from the altar, I could see some of the congregation in the organ loft reading the *Cork Weekly Examiner*, and curls of cigarette smoke rising into the air.

To see if they were listening, I once preached, 'I wonder what you'd think if someone were to come from the back of the church, tap you on the shoulder and tell you that you were going to die in 30 minutes.'

All the papers suddenly went down and they listened intently, before leaving church for the pub opposite, nicknamed the Vatican Arms.

But I knew I couldn't continue to work with the parish priest. I went to see the Bishop.

'It's hopeless,' I said. 'I can't get on with him. He drinks, he swears and he belches.'

The Bishop said that he could understand the drinking, but that swearing and belching were not good and that he would move me.

On my last Sunday, the priest proclaimed at length that everyone coming out of the seminary was a 'booger' and he was glad I was going – and that the Vatican Council had been called by the devil!

We finally got to the end of the service.

'The Mass is ended, go forth in peace,' he said.

A broad Irish voice came from the back, 'And not before time.'

After 13 weeks in Deptford, I was moved to St Bede's, Clapham Park, where I shared the presbytery with the parish priest, Father Salmon, and a Dutchman called Father Bodewes, a retired missionary, who was a nice man but an alcoholic.

One of my most important roles at St Bede's was with the church's young people. I appointed the youth club leaders, who were fabulous, and we took the club abroad several times.

On our last night in the Austrian village of Arzl – you can imagine what the boys called it! – Tony, Daphne and I were playing cards while the youngsters had gone into Innsbruck. The next day on the train the kids were all giggling and we knew that something was up. They confessed that the night before they had turned round all the signposts.

As well as being chaplain to our club, I served for some time on the Borough of Lambeth Youth Committee.

I spent a lot of time in the local schools – where they got to know that I had a liking for Inner London Education Authority custard. (I still think it's the best!) I would get a message from the kitchens when it was on the menu, and they'd save a bowl for me.

It was during my time at St Bede's that I was asked to become Deputy RC Priest at Brixton Prison, visiting weekly and standing in for the full-time priest when he was away. This was an interesting experience – and doubtless contributed to my (future) decision to become a probation officer. The inmates were either on remand, or serving short sentences. Most of the staff I encountered were really lovely people, and the majority of the prisoners were, too. The more challenging inmates were those in the psychiatric 'B' wing.

On one occasion when I visited, I was informed by the senior member of staff that they had Jesus in one of the cells, and that he was sure that the man would love to see me. When we got to his cell, the staff member asked the man, 'Who are you?' 'Jesus,' the man replied. 'Who sent you, then?' 'God sent me,' was the reply. From the next cell, the inmate called out, 'No I bloody didn't!'

My grandparents had given me an Austin Mini Van on the occasion of my ordination to the priesthood. One day it was stolen from its usual place outside the house, along with my sick-call set for my ministry to the unwell, which I had left inside. The insurance company paid up quickly, and I replaced the van with a similar one. As for the sick-call set, someone must have had a guilty conscience, as the set, which was hand-made by a friend at the seminary, re-appeared on the doorstep a few days later.

We had a very good choir at St Bede's, led by our organist, Peter, who was just 12 years old. I made friends with many of them. One of the members, an unmarried woman a few years my senior, invited me for a meal at her home in Balham. I can't recall how it happened, but we landed up in bed together. It was there that I lost my virginity. I felt very guilty about it and went to confession – anonymously – at Westminster Cathedral shortly afterwards.

My downfall at St Bede's came when I was asked to write an article for an underground magazine about the church's attitude to gay people. I had several gay friends and felt that many of them were treated abominably by their churches, and especially the Roman Catholic Church. For this reason, I had been involved for a couple of years in the Campaign for Homosexual Equality. I also provided counsel to gay men at the Anglican centre in Marylebone known as the Centre Counselling Trust.

My article was entitled 'One priest and the homosexual', the gist of it being that the Catholic Church is very good at moral theology – except when it comes to sex, where it resorts to short-cuts and threats of hellfire. One evening about 50 copies of the magazine were delivered during supper. Father Salmon was furious when he read it. Ironically, Father Salmon was a closet homosexual himself – I was well aware that he entertained young men in his rooms on the floor below me in the presbytery.

As a result of my article, on 11th February 1971 I was summoned to see Cyril Cowderoy, who was now Archbishop of Southwark. He ranted on about what 'nasty filthy dirty people' homosexuals were.

I told him I couldn't see how his attitude reflected the compassion of Jesus towards people like the Prodigal Son and the woman who committed adultery.

The Archbishop was furious. He stood up behind his desk.

'Who are you to teach me the scriptures, you impudent young man,' he boomed.

Father Salmon wanted rid of me, and that was how I found myself in Sevenoaks – and began to find my calling to the Catholic Church challenged.

5. SEVENOAKS AND THE CHARISMATIC RENEWAL (1971-1973)

Sevenoaks was a big parish, carved up into areas for which one priest took responsibility. The parish priest, Father Donnelly, did all the weddings and funerals, but the rest of us had duty days on which we had to be available in case someone wanted to talk to a priest. Father Donnelly lived next door to the presbytery, which I shared with two other priests: Paddy Pearson and Kevin Pelham, known as 'Ron'. Ron taught in a church school at Hildenborough, a few miles away.

Father Pearson and I fell out for some reason I never understood, so instead of speaking to me, he used to leave me little notes. But Ron and I got on very well. When he moved, there was a gap in the school staff for teaching RE at CSE level (the former qualification a grade below 'O' level) and the headmaster asked if I'd be prepared to take it on.

'The only thing is, you've got two terms to get through two years' work.'

I said I'd accept the challenge – but insisted on double periods. In the first period we ploughed through St Luke's Gospel, and in the second, undertook a project on homelessness, and visited the Cyrenians' place near Canterbury. I was delighted when all of my group passed. One of them even went off to be a missionary in later life.

Sevenoaks is an affluent town, and we had several millionaires in our parish. One wonderful couple, John and Gay Leonard, had a swimming pool and tennis court, and often invited me to their home for meals.

It was while I was in Sevenoaks that I was introduced to the Charismatic Renewal movement. I was becoming increasingly disillusioned with the Catholic Church, partly because of the birth control issue, but also because I found the church too conservative. A friend invited me to see this different aspect of Catholicism, which was headed by Bronwen Astor, widow of the third Viscount Astor and former mistress of Cliveden, the house famous for its part in the Profumo affair. Bronwen now lived in Tuesley Manor in Godalming, which was where the Charismatic Renewal meetings took place. Soon, I was going regularly. Through Charismatic Renewal I was baptised in the Spirit – by the laying on of hands – which was all completely new to me.

I guess it was my exposure to this movement – with its focus on expressing the gifts of the Holy Spirit – that gradually led me away from (Roman) Catholicism. I had started Bible studies at Mabledon, an Anglican retreat house nearby, which also enlarged my vision.

I was once invited to lunch at Bronwen's, where two medium-sized roasted chickens somehow served about 20 guests, with more than enough for us all to have second helpings. It reminds me of the story of St John Vianney, also known as the Curé d'Ars, in the nineteenth century. He was chaplain to an orphanage, where, one night, the Reverend Mother said to him, 'We're running out of grain.'

'Don't worry, go to sleep,' he replied.

And the next morning, the granary was full.

Sometimes we don't believe miracles, even when they happen right in front of our eyes. We say, 'Come, Holy Spirit!' yet don't really expect him to come. If we did, life would be far more exciting!

I was once again involved in youth work. It was through my friendship with Kevin, a member of our senior youth club and the son of an Anglican clergyman, that I witnessed another extraordinary occurrence.

Kevin had gone to his doctor about an injury on his foot, which he thought was from playing rugby. Sadly it turned out to be cancer, and poor Kevin eventually had his leg amputated. He often hobbled up to my room at the top of the presbytery on my duty day, where we'd keep each other company.

One day he said to me, out of the blue, 'Francis, I want you to conduct my funeral.'

I agreed, and we changed the subject.

I supported Kevin in his final days, and was with him when he passed away at home, at the age of 21. Just before he died, although all the windows and doors of the room were closed, a sudden swirling – a kind of breeze – circled above Kevin as he lay in his bed. I often think about this at Pentecost, with the rushing wind and the tongues of fire and the Holy Spirit filling the disciples.

In May 1973 I wrote another article, 'Homosexuality and the Churches', this time for *The Spectator*, and assuming the name Peter Storey. It was essentially an interview with Lord Donald Soper, leader of the Methodist church at the time, who was pushing for greater understanding of homosexuality and taking a more sympathetic stance from that of his contemporaries in the mainstream Christian churches.

I knew that my time in the Catholic Church had come to an end. I wrote to the Archbishop informing him of my decision. He wasn't happy. I had to see the Suffragan Bishop, who told me to write a letter to the Pope, asking for dispensation. Before I left, he asked me to solemnly swear that I would not give any interviews to the media.

'I intend to cause scandal to no one,' I assured him, 'but I won't swear to that.'

On discovering that I had come by train, Canon Denning, who was Chancellor of the diocese, offered to drive me home. Every five minutes, he'd say to me, 'You will swear, won't you?'

The more he asked, the more adamant I became.

6. PROBATION SERVICE (1973-1975)

The traumatic time that followed my leaving the priesthood was helped considerably by a kind offer from John Leonard, who gave me the use of his late mother's house in Yarmouth on the Isle of Wight while I contemplated my future.

While I was in Sevenoaks I had met Greet, from Breda in the Netherlands, who had been working as an au pair for Bronwen Astor. I made a lot of phone calls to Greet from the island, and she came to stay a couple of times. We were becoming close. I also spent a lot of time travelling around by bus and sitting looking out to sea, as well as watching TV and reading.

One night I got quite depressed and thought I'd commit suicide by throwing myself from the promontory into the Solent. I wandered down there, thought, 'It looks a bit cold,' and went home and had a hot bath instead. The next morning, I felt fine again.

I visited Quarr Abbey a few times, where on one occasion I caught up unexpectedly with an old friend, Alan Rees, whom I had first met in about 1960 at the Society of St Gregory, which specialised in church music. We were both staying in the guest wing at the abbey, but the guest master forgot to allocate me a room with a bed. Alan suggested that I sleep on the floor in his room, and kindly gave me some of his blankets – the result being that we both froze. To keep warm, we ended up in the single bed together. Needless to say, the guest master was hugely embarrassed the next morning! Alan eventually became a monk and, later still, Abbot at Belmont. Very sadly, suffering from acute depression, he took his own life in 2005.

I had decided to become a probation officer, and duly sent off my application. After undertaking psychological and mathematical tests along with several other candidates, I was interviewed by a Lady Harris, who asked, 'Do you think you're a latent adolescent?'

'Probably', I replied, to which she said, 'I'm glad you're not one of these complicated religious people, but just a naughty boy.' It was all rather patronising.

Only two out of our group of 11 were accepted for training on what would be the last Home Office one-year course leading to the Certificate of Qualification in Social Work (CQSW).

My training began in September 1973 with three months in Walthamstow, working with an experienced probation officer. I was living at the time in the house of a friend in Croydon, and commuted on the Victoria line some days and stayed in the YMCA on others. Greet and I were a couple by then, and I remember smuggling her into the hostel, which was strictly against the rules!

The on-the-job training was followed by a four-month course at the Home Office training centre in Cromwell Road, followed by four months at their training centre in

Wandsworth, where my individual tutor was a man called Mark.

The criminology lecturer at Cromwell Road recommended we read 37 books in three months! No way was I going to manage that, but in the exam I quoted from a selection of the books, giving the impression I'd read them – and managed to get a grade A.

During my time at Wandsworth, I was attached to the South West Magistrates Court in Battersea, where the stipendiary magistrate was Mr Louden. Anybody who came in front of him who had stolen a car was sent to Borstal automatically because his wife had been injured by a joyrider. Interestingly, I became known as a hard-line probation officer myself because I'd recommend the detention centre at Send for some of the kids, reasoning that a short sharp shock would put them on the straight and narrow. Usually, it worked – it was simply a case of getting them in time.

The Assistant Chief Probation Officer, Jane Hill, offered me a job back in Walthamstow, along with a council flat, provided I was married. Rather hurriedly, Greet and I tied the knot in Croydon registry office in February 1974. But in June we had a church wedding, taken by the prior of Quarr Abbey, Dom Joe Warrilow. We celebrated afterwards in a restaurant in Cobham, hosted by Greet's father.

Our new home in Walthamstow was a fourth-floor flat in Northwood Tower, a 20-storey block overlooking Wood Street railway station. It wasn't the most salubrious area, but we were happy, the two of us and our cat. We once made the mistake of leaving pork chops out to thaw and coming home to find they'd all gone – and the cat with a smile on its face! At weekends we would sit out on the balcony overlooking the station with a bottle of cider, the only luxury we could afford.

Work was good, and I like to think I made a difference. One of my tasks as a probation officer was to write Social Enquiry Reports – making a recommendation to the magistrates about an appropriate penalty for the offenders. I particularly remember Jonathan, a young man who had been caught committing an indecent act. I recommended a money payment supervision order, which meant Jonathan would come and see me every week, while paying off his £100-pound fine in instalments. All was going well until the fines officer rang to tell me he had stopped paying at £95. I asked Jonathan why, and was touched when he replied, 'I didn't want to stop coming to see you.'

'Pay it off,' I said, 'and I'll put you on voluntary supervision.' This meant we could continue our meetings.

When our son Egon – later known as Billy – was born in 1975, Jonathan designed a card with a stork on the front for us to send to our friends. He was just one of the lovely people I met while I was in Walthamstow.

Billy cried every evening between 4.30 and 6.30 – and the reinforced concrete of the tower block vibrated. Greet and I had no experience of babies, and invited my old schoolfriend, Gerald, who was a local paediatrician, for a meal – and to see what he could recommend for the crying.

'He's got very good lungs, hasn't he,' was Gerald's only comment.

One day I saw an advert for a Senior Probation Officer/Warden of a probation hostel in Beckenham that hadn't yet opened. Although I had only been qualified for 16 months, I decided to apply. I was interviewed by Harry Hilton, the Chief Probation Officer of South East London. He was particularly impressed by my idea of looking at biorhythms, and whether they affected criminality.

I was offered the job.

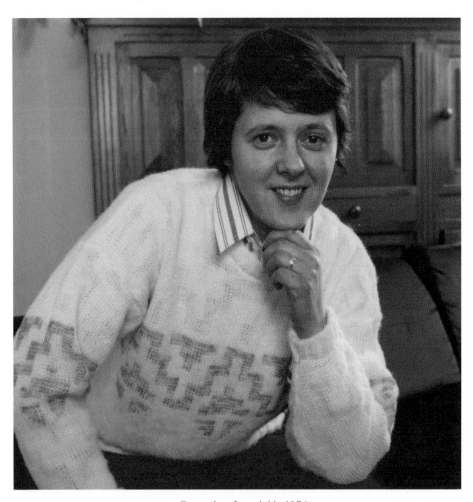

Greet, whom I married in 1974

7. THE HOSTEL (1975-1977)

It was October 1975, and the hostel was due to open in January 1976. I had three months to oversee the whole thing coming together, from the arrival of furniture to the appointment of staff. In an interesting reversal of roles, Mark – who had been my training boss in Wandsworth – became my deputy, and we had two assistants, Margaret and Stephen. Greet, Billy and I lived in a flat above the hostel.

It was an Approved Probation Hostel, for residents who had mental health problems rather than being out-and-out criminals. One common factor was a broken home. We would have a session once a week when a psychiatrist from the Maudsley Hospital came to observe the group dynamics, followed by a staff debrief.

As I'd mentioned it in my interview, I did also look into biorhythms and possible links with criminality, but the results were unconvincing.

Our residents were an interesting bunch. One of them, Keith, liked to grease his hair, but instead of Brylcreme he used margarine – and stank! With my agreement, some of the residents stripped him down and put him in the bath. Another man, Terry, was too ill for the psychiatric unit (!) so came to us instead with his medication. He used to barricade himself in his bedroom and talk to little green people from Mars! He once threatened me with a broken bottle. It wasn't uncommon for me to hear a noise somewhere and have to go and break up a fight.

Our management committee sometimes joined us for the evening meal. A magistrate at Bromley used to talk about her pussy, which, as you can imagine, gave rise to stifled giggles.

In the notorious hot summer of 1976, when Fred the chef was away on leave, Greet bravely took over the cooking. Preparing hot meals in an already steamy kitchen was quite a challenge.

One day I went into the back garden and saw what looked like a freshly dug grave.

'Who's that for?' I asked David, to which he replied, 'It's for you.'

'Be a good chap and fill it in.'

Which he did without a murmur.

I'm still in touch with my first resident, Bob. I used to leave my study door open most of the time, and one day noticed him pacing up and down the corridor.

'What's up, Bob?'

He came into the room and sat down.

'I think I'm gay.'

'So?'

'Well, don't you mind?'

'Not if you don't.'

I later saw Bob through a couple of relationships. He's now teaching English in Thailand, and we remain friends.

In the first year, the reconviction rate of our nine residents was nil. Mark and I were very selective about whom we recommended for the hostel, which doubtless had something to do with it. But the Home Office got stroppy and insisted we take others, and that's when a little re-offending took place.

I had to admire the ingenuity of one of these offences. One of the residents climbed onto the flat roof of the men's outfitters opposite the hostel, opened up the hatch and let down a fishing rod, managing to 'catch' himself a few suits and bypass the alarm. He was eventually caught and sent to prison.

In 1977, our second child, Ben, was born. When someone started throwing stones at the window of our flat, just missing Ben's cot, I knew we couldn't stay. We had bought a house in Shirley, part of Croydon, and we decided to move there. I devised a rota for night duty. My deputy said he couldn't stay at night for personal reasons, so the assistant wardens and I took it in turns. The outcome was that I was suspended for not insisting that Mark do his share. However, as it wasn't in his contract, I could not enforce it.

I was reinstated without censure, but it was really a pyrrhic victory and I could no longer see myself working for that committee.

'Why don't you go back into the field?' suggested Harry Hilton.

So later that year, I did just that. My patch covered New Addington, Selsdon and Monks Hill, and our office was in Mint Walk, Croydon.

As a probation officer you meet nice people who have done terrible things. One of my clients was a man who had been imprisoned for killing his baby. The baby just cried and cried. He eventually 'lost it' and shook the baby so hard that he killed it. He was very remorseful.

Sometimes you can't help liking people, no matter what they've done.

The probation hostel in Beckenham

8. THE ROAD TO ANGLICANISM (1973-1979)

n 1973, just before going to train in Walthamstow, I had been to talk to the Anglican Bishop of Croydon, John Hughes. Leaving the Catholic Church had made me aware of a hole in my life that I needed to fill. I had been to a few Quaker meetings, to fill the Sunday 'gap', but I felt that I needed something with more structure.

'We don't want to have you on the rebound,' said the Bishop. But he encouraged me to think about it further.

When I got the job in Walthamstow – and following a colleague who had been a (RC) Passionist father but was now an Anglican priest – I went to see John Trillo, the Bishop of Chelmsford.

'I think you'd be good and that we can use the gifts you've got,' he said. 'I just need some references.'

Some time later I received a letter from him saying that he was sorry not to be able to take things further, but that I was welcome to go and see him. When I did so, I saw a letter on his desk with the Archbishop of Southwark's crest on top. Bearing in mind the way the Archbishop and I had parted company, this was ominous.

But I was still taken aback when Bishop Trillo asked me, 'Is it true that you got a girl pregnant in one of your parishes?'

Horrified, I replied, 'Absolutely not. I'll swear on the Bible if you want me to.'

I had no idea where such a story had come from. I had been chaplain of a convent school whilst at St Bede's, but all friendships had been of a strictly platonic nature.

The Bishop was happy with my explanation. He said that he saw no problem in having me licensed, but first he suggested I see Canon Douglas Webster at St Paul's Cathedral – 'to get the other bias,' as he put it.

Canon Webster and I hit it off immediately. In our hour-long meetings, we spent 50 minutes chatting about the church, and the remaining 10 looking at a book he'd recommended. After the second meeting – as he sucked on his favourite sugared almonds – he said, 'It's lovely seeing you, but this is a bit of a waste of your time and mine, isn't it?' I then had to go through something called the Colonial Clergy Act before being signed off by Archbishop Donald Coggan.

I was received in the Anglican church at a service officiated by Bishop Trillo in July 1975.

'Do you wish to become a member of the Church of England?'

'Yes I do.'

'Welcome to the Church of England!'

And that was it, along with a prayer.

For my licensing, in November of that year, I had to affirm my allegiance to the catholic creeds and acknowledge the *Book of Common Prayer* – 'as a historical document will do,' whispered Bishop Trillo.

And finally: 'Francis, do you promise allegiance to all things lawful and good? And Francis [another whisper], that gives you a lot of leeway, you know.'

I made my promise.

I became a non-stipendiary priest (NSM) at St Peter in the Forest, one of the Walthamstow churches. Then, when I moved to the hostel, helped out Paul Longbottom, a vicar and friend at Holy Trinity Beckenham, whom I'd known when I was a curate in Sevenoaks. I stayed there until I moved to Shirley, where I became NSM for the parish of St John's, and its vicar, Arthur Quinn. He and I worked well together.

In a way, Arthur was partly responsible for the next stage of my life. One day he mentioned a society which offered free holidays for clergy in Europe in return for some pastoral duties. The society was called the Commonwealth and Continental Church Society – nicknamed 'Com and Con' (and today renamed the Intercontinental Church Society, or ICS). I rang to get some details and in their reply they enclosed a book entitled *Something Happened at The Hague*. The accompanying letter said that if I wanted to keep the book, it would cost me 75p. I put the book aside and popped a cheque in the post.

When Greet went to visit her family in Holland that Christmas, I came across the book. I devoured it from cover to cover in one sitting. It had been written by John Lewis, chaplain at the Embassy church in The Hague, and was all about church renewal there. Two days later, I saw an advert in the *Church Times* for an associate chaplain in the city. This felt more than coincidental: God-incidental, rather!

I didn't really fit the description of the person they were looking for. The Com and Con was an evangelical society, whereas my background was Catholic. Nevertheless, I applied and was invited for an interview at the London HQ. Curiously, and again God-incidentally, just before my interview John Lewis was visiting the Royal School of Church Music – about a mile from where I lived – with his choir. We met and 'clicked' immediately. Within days of my interview I was informed that it had been unanimously agreed that I should be appointed.

However, before my appointment could be finalised I had to meet the Bishop in Europe, John Satterthwaite. He said there were a number of issues which needed to be resolved in The Hague. Charismatic Renewal had caused a division in the congregation between those who had been baptised in the Spirit – and were perhaps speaking in tongues – and those who had not, with the former believing themselves to be superior to the latter. The Bishop felt that I was the right person to tackle this problem.

On 17th June 1979, Greet, Billy, Ben and I left Croydon for a new life in the Netherlands.

9. LIFE IN THE HAGUE (1979-1983)

My official title was Associate Chaplain to the English and American Episcopal Church, but John wanted me to be in charge of the new, experimental church in Voorschoten, which was home to the British School in the Netherlands.

My area covered the whole of the north of The Hague, up to the border of the Amsterdam chaplaincy, including Voorschoten, the lovely seaside port of Nordwijk, and Lisse, with its famous Keukenhof gardens. John covered the southern part, including the beautiful city of Delft, to the border of Rotterdam.

Voorschoten was an interesting place. Thanks to the school, it was attracting more and more expatriates. We held a service in the school's music room every Sunday, attended by around 25 to 30 people. The railway line ran just outside the window. If the 'D' train from Amsterdam to Paris went by when I was still preaching, you'd hear the sudden clearing of throats – as it meant I had been speaking for too long. It was all very informal. I became school counsellor there for both staff and students.

One of the things I did at the school – in cooperation with the head of sixth form – was introduce a course called Community Education. I was aware that these expat kids lived in a kind of bubble, and needed to know what life was like outside it. One of the tasks we set them was writing formal letters, for example, how to book a room in a hotel. Their letters were rubbish – they hadn't got a clue!

One of my pupils, Christoph, was the son of the Austrian ambassador. With our shared heritage, we took to each other immediately, and I was honoured to be invited to meet his parents. Christoph is now an ambassador himself!

It was in the British School that I was presented – with others from the expatriate community – to Princess Margaret, who was visiting The Hague. I remember that she looked completely bored, and that her eyes were humourless.

Being chaplain to the Embassy church meant being invited to various official functions.

At one British Embassy function I noticed a man on his own in the corner. I introduced myself.

'I'm from the Russian Embassy,' replied the stranger.

We chatted all evening about theism, politics, the Dutch – in fact just about everything under the sun. As I was leaving, the Number two at the British Embassy approached me and said, 'See you in my office tomorrow morning at ten.'

When I asked him why, he replied, 'You've been talking to the Russian all evening. You need to come for a debrief.'

I refused point blank.

The Ambassador, Philip Mansfield, told me to take no notice of him. I don't think he had a very high opinion of his deputy, who used to wear red, white and blue everything – right down to his socks and his handkerchief.

We all liked living in The Hague. Billy went to the local Dutch school and Ben to an English nursery. Greet and I had a favourite restaurant we frequented when we could get a babysitter.

The very particular Dutch woman who lived next door used to put her duvet over the railings to air every morning, and cut her grass with scissors. Needless to say, neither she nor Greet and I were amused when our boys spray-painted her front door one day . . .

I got on incredibly well with John, my boss. With his help, I succeeded in stamping out the first- and second-class citizen approach that had divided the church on my arrival.

When, in 1982, John was promoted to Archdeacon of North-West Europe and moved to Brussels, I covered the interregnum.

The Ambassador wanted me to take over the job permanently, but the General Secretary of the Com and Con owed someone a favour. His appointee was a very conservative Ulster Protestant. I couldn't cope with him at all. If he heard me preach, he would say later, 'I would have said this instead,' and proceed to lecture me on where he thought I had gone wrong.

Once, I rang to tell him that Greet and I both had flu.

'Francis, how did you get flu?' he asked me.

I explained that there was a bug going round the British School.

'No, Francis,' he replied, 'unforgiven sin.'

I stayed for about a year after his appointment, but we were on totally different wavelengths. The Bishop of Croydon had told me to get in touch when I was ready to return, so I duly dropped him a line.

I heard nothing for a while and then got a phone call telling me that a South London parish had a vacancy for a vicar. Greet and I hopped on a boat back to England and found ourselves at St Stephen's Church in Norbury.

It can only be said that St Stephen's was a mess. We visited incognito for a service, where one priest preached through the screen and another lay across the high altar steps during the intercessions, his arms outstretched. It was very bizarre!

'What do you think?' I asked Greet.

She replied, 'It's so awful, I think God's telling us to come here.'

I had to agree with her.

The next day I had an interview with the Bishop.

'When can you start?' he asked.

10. ST STEPHEN'S, NORBURY AND THORNTON HEATH (1983-2000)

We took the overnight ferry from Holland and arrived back in the UK on 7th April 1983.

Our new home was a 1960s vicarage behind the church. There was so much rubbish in and around the church that we had a bonfire in our large garden every night for about three weeks after our arrival.

On my first Sunday, I introduced a nave altar, which drew some criticism as I hadn't told anyone what I intended to do. A complaint went to the Bishop and to the Commissary General for the diocese of Canterbury – the judge of the consistory court – who came to have a look.

As one looked up the church, on the left-hand side there was a so-called memorial altar with a grey hardboard backing. It was so awful that whenever I walked past it, I gave it a kick from the back.

'What's that thing?' the Commissary General asked me. 'It's dreadful. Take it out.'

He approved of everything I was doing, but said I would have to get a faculty – required for any material alteration in a church or churchyard – in due course. I must have got myself a bit of a reputation for changing things as, whenever he came to visit, the first thing Archdeacon Fred Hazell would say, was, 'Francis, what have you done that I shouldn't know about?!'

At my interview, the Bishop had warned me that my predecessor had been knocked out by some yobs who were sitting on a wall outside the church. As they had told him they did it because they were bored, the Bishop had promised to start a youth club for them. So, one of my first challenges was to fulfil that promise, helped by a youth leader from Croydon council. The young troublemakers duly appeared, stayed for a while, then drifted off again. We had a separate youth club for church members.

I had lots of enthusiastic parishioners at St Stephen's. These included a couple of men, who were very involved in the church: Andrew chaired the Pastoral Care and Outreach Committee, while David, his partner, was my parish MC and PCC Secretary (and has since been ordained and is now Vicar of Mitcham). Their arrival in the parish had caused a certain amount of 'chit- chat', but I pointed out that another member of the congregation was a spinster who shared a house with a female friend. How did we know that their relationship wasn't purely platonic?

One of my parishioners, Graham, was an architect, and he designed a nave altar on an octagonal plinth so that we could arrange the chairs more or less in the round. We financed that by asking people to pay for a piece of wood on which we wrote their name, before it was all covered over by a new carpet. The altar itself was refurbished by Mark Hendy, a wonderful man.

About five years after my arrival, I felt we were stagnating, and fell into a depression. The Archdeacon, who had been tipped off about my condition, rang me up one day, and said, 'Francis, I want to take you out for lunch.' He took me to one of the best hotels in Croydon for a slap-up meal.

Very soon afterwards I began to feel more positive about everything. I knew I had the Archdeacon's full support, as well as that of Stuart Snell, the evangelical Bishop of Croydon. But I also put my recovery down to the very good people at St Stephen's. A congregation willing to take over the roles that need filling and carry them out efficiently and with goodwill is a godsend to any priest.

Opposite the church there had been a convent which, during my time, was razed and replaced with a block of flats. One new tenant rang me to complain about the bell, which was rung at 7.55, calling people to worship at our 8 a.m. service. I had to tell him that the bell had been rung every Sunday at that time since 1909, when the church was built! After that there were no more complaints.

Over time, my congregation began to include more and more people of West Indian descent. By the time I left, I would estimate that sixty per cent of my congregation was non-white. Bishop Snell was succeeded by the Church of England's first black bishop, Wilfred Wood, who said to me one day, 'Francis, if they didn't like you, they wouldn't stay.'

We started the use of name labels in church. With roughly a hundred people for the main service, it meant that we could see who had been in church and who hadn't. If people were missing for three weeks, we would ring them to ensure they were OK.

Once a month we held a Holy Communion service with the ministry of healing. One of our regular parishioners, Barbara, had cancer. She came to church one Sunday evening before being admitted to hospital for a major operation the following day. My colleague and I laid hands on her, and I remember her back getting hotter and hotter, to the point where I had to remove them.

The next day, the surgeon told Barbara he would like to take a few more X-rays before the operation. Two hours later, he told his astonished patient, 'You can go home. There's no trace of cancer.'

Not everyone who receives God's healing power does so as humbly as Barbara did. One morning after the midweek service, a lady came into church and said rather aggressively, 'You Father Pole?' I confirmed that I was. 'It's my leg, isn't it?' I asked what the problem was. 'Well, it won't heal up, will it?' I suggested we find a quiet place to talk about it.

We went into the Lady Chapel and sat down.

'Have you been to the doctor?'

'Yes, but he can't do anything.'

I asked her what had been going on in her life, and learnt that her husband had died.

'How do you feel about that?'

'Very angry'.

There were some other issues too, but clearly that was the main one. I suggested we pray about it, and embarked on a sort of blunderbuss prayer that covered most things. That seemed to satisfy her and off she went.

Meanwhile, one of my parishioners, Wilma Roest, had decided to buy a flat and wanted to show it to Greet and myself. The door of the flat was opened by the woman I had prayed with. Coincidentally, it was her home that Wilma was buying.

She greeted me with, 'You're Father Pole – you're the one who healed my leg.'

To which I replied, 'God actually did it. I just prayed. What happened?'

'It got better, didn't it?'

Another example of the healing power of prayer.

Wilma is now Vicar of Richmond and a canon, and along with David, one of several of my parishioners who found or developed their vocations at St Stephen's. Joyce Forbes, who was born in Jamaica, is another. Joyce was a social worker in Brixton when I met her, went on to be ordained, and is now a canon.

I said to her one day, when she was considering her vocation, 'When you get on God's train, you can't get off and you won't know where you're going. But it's OK!'

Some of my congregation trained as Readers. One of them, Ray Wheeler, is now Diocesan Warden of Readers. Others found their calling in different ways. It's just a case of seeing where people's talents lie, and nurturing them.

Meanwhile, I had been serving on both the Diocesan and Archdeaconry Pastoral Committees, but left the former as the committee refused to take seriously the beginning of the HIV/AIDS epidemic. I had attended seminars on the subject, led by hospital consultants, and knew how worried the medical establishment was. I took one of the first funerals of an AIDS victim, but because the disease was relatively new, I had to disguise the cause of his death. Some relatives and friends actually thought he had died of cancer. Several years later I lost a friend, Robert, to AIDS.

I also took part in several question-and-answer sessions on local radio. Following a letter to *The Times* regarding the increasing incidence of drugs, I was invited to take part in a discussion on ITV where one of the other participants was the singer Boy George!

I first met Simon Evans in 1977 when I was an NSM in Shirley and he was a member of the choir and youth club. I had been delighted when – after a career in banking – he decided to be ordained. Having been promised a curate, I asked the Bishop if I could have Simon. He was rather hesitant, but Archbishop Robert Runcie thought it was a splendid idea to appoint someone I already counted as a friend. And so Simon was my curate at St Stephen's for four years. Today he is a vicar in Bournemouth and in 2022 was made a canon of Salisbury Cathedral. We remain great friends and meet whenever we can.

Simon and I co-led pilgrimages to the Holy Land while we were at St Stephen's. I well and truly got the bug for the Holy Land the very first time I went there – on a familiarisation trip that cost me just sixty pounds – and have been six times. I love the place, for its churches and its history, bringing me closer to the Jesus of the Bible. But my visits have rarely been without incident. On one occasion, our party had to be diverted after an incendiary device was found in the road. Another time we were unable to visit Jericho because crowds had been throwing stones at the (Palestinian) coaches that we used. Shortly after that very first visit, some Arabs blew themselves up in the hotel we had been staying in. None of these incidents put me off – in fact, I returned several times afterwards.

My father died in 1988, several years after a stroke left him paralysed. He had no fear of death. 'I'm a Christian: I know where I'm going,' he said, refusing antibiotics for the pneumonia that killed him. In 1982, he had published his autobiography, *Two Halves of a Life*, detailing his journey from Austria to Kent and the life he made for himself and our family in England.

My widowed mother came to live round the corner from St Stephen's, where she cheerfully attended Anglican services, despite being a Catholic. In her new home, she enjoyed the luxury of central heating for the first time in her life, my father having never approved of it! She died in Croydon in 2006.

Meanwhile, in our own household, Billy had been getting jealous of his younger brother, so we sent him as a weekly boarder to The Hawthorns, an independent school in Bletchingley. Greet had been against the idea, but it proved the right move for Billy and he enjoyed his time there enormously. Later, after a spell at St John's School, Leatherhead, he joined Ben at St Andrew's, a local Church of England secondary school.

Greet and I were forever being summoned to the school for Ben's misdemeanours. He got on well with his deputy head, who told him once, 'Ben, if you don't work, you'll end up stacking shelves in Tesco.' Which, at one point he did – before going on to the local sixth-form college.

Although our two boys were very different, and could sometimes be quite aggressive towards each other, in time they became the best of friends, and they remain close today.

Holy place: Nicky, Emily and Katie at the Western Wall, Jerusalem

*Renewal of baptismal vows: Simon and me with Katie, in the River Jordan. Nicky
and Simon's son, James, are behind*

St Stephen's

11. POLICE CHAPLAINCY (1987-2021)

One day in 1987 I got a phone call from the Archdeacon.

'We're thinking of starting a police chaplaincy south of the river. As a former probation officer, would you be interested in getting involved?'

It began with 14 of us within our diocese of Southwark – a mix of Anglicans, Baptists and Methodists. North of the Thames there was just one chaplain.

When I went to see the chief superintendent, Sally Hubbard, at Norbury police station, she said, 'It might take up to five years for them to accept you, but if you betray a confidence, you'll be out in five minutes.'

You see all sides of humanity when you are in patrol cars with the police. On one occasion, we went to a house where someone had been dialling 999 and then putting the receiver down. This had happened a few times and there was concern that the caller was afraid to speak. It turned out to be a man who was being threatened by his own son. When we arrived, the son – a great big fellow – got up and thumped one of the two officers I was with. They duly arrested him and I had to give evidence in court.

In 1990 we held our first national conference at the Police Staff College in Bramshill in Hampshire, with approximately

30 chaplains; we made the decision to meet every other year. I looked for a different venue in 1994 when it was clear that we were outgrowing Bramshill, and discovered the Hayes Conference Centre in Derbyshire. In 1996 I became Secretary of our National Association of Police Chaplains, and four years later National Coordinator, the previous one having resigned. I held the post for several years, until I was succeeded by Bill Hopley, a very popular man and Senior Chaplain to West Midlands Police, who sadly died of cancer shortly afterwards.

For several years I went to the American conference training weeks. The first was in Birmingham, Alabama. I also attended conferences in San Jose (California), Duluth (Minnesota), Albuquerque (New Mexico) and Notre Dame (Indiana). I became European representative of the organisation as well. I'd beg for whatever grants I could to finance my trips.

In 1998 I used my training and experience to write a handbook for police chaplains, which was funded by the Met. I used it as my thesis to become Certified Master Chaplain (CMC) in the USA.

One special memory is of my time at St Stephen's when I acted as chaplain to Speaker of the House of Commons, Bernard Weatherill, who was a Croydon MP. On 3rd May 1991 I took part in the Speaker's procession and led prayers in the House. I treasure a note of thanks from him, written on a copy of the prayers.

I was at St Stephen's for 17 years, and I think that I might well have stayed there, and not come to Crawley, if my wife had not left me in 1999 after she fell in love with Julia.

When I went to see the Bishop, he suggested I think about a change of ministry. 'You've been a good parish priest for 17 years, but perhaps you should keep an open mind as to whether you continue in parish ministry or take on a different role.'

One day in November, three months after Greet moved out, I was chairing a meeting of police chaplains at Heathrow when one of them stood up. He said if anyone was interested in a job that combined 20 per cent parish work and 80 per cent as Industrial Chaplain, to get in touch. As I drove home, I found myself thinking about what he had said.

I gave him a call. 'Where is this job?'

'Crawley, a new town in West Sussex. If you're interested, ring the Archdeacon of Horsham.'

I rang William Filby the following morning. He thought I sounded like the sort of person they were looking for, and arranged a meeting for me with the Bishop of Horsham, Lindsay Urwin. I learnt that the job was to be a Team Vicar of the Crawley Town Centre parish. Each of the five churches had its own Team Vicar, and I would be located at St Michael and All Angels in Lowfield Heath, on the edge of Gatwick Airport.

Bishop Lindsay was happy to appoint me, subject to DBS checks and references from the police. Everything happened very quickly after that. The Bishop said that he would announce my appointment on 16th January 2000. The boys had both left home by now and were living independent lives in Croydon. I was therefore on my own when I moved into the house in Langley Green, the home for industrial chaplains.

12. CRAWLEY (2000-PRESENT DAY)

was struck by the leafiness as you entered the town. Crawley looked far greener than I remembered from a previous visit. The main drawback to my appointment was that the house needed a lot of work, having been empty for two and a half years.

I was licensed on 20th May 2000 at St Michael's, Lowfield Heath, on a particularly foggy evening. The village of Lowfield Heath had long since been swallowed up by Gatwick Airport, and there were few residents left. When planes took off to the east, I had to stop preaching because of the noise. When I first arrived, there were 17 in the congregation in the winter and as few as six in the summer. St Michael's Church was essentially propped up by the Thomas Mason Trust, which I soon felt was not a good use of trust money. We voted – with the agreement of Rector Malcolm Liles – to close the church in 2002.

I moved to St Elizabeth's, another of the team churches, and stayed until that church too closed, as it was no longer financially viable. It was there that I became friendly with Nicky, who used to come to church with her little daughters, Emily and Katie. Nicky, a primary school teacher, was in the process of leaving her husband, and needed a place to stay. I happened to have bought a house in Malthouse Road in Crawley for my retirement, using inheritance money, and I suggested she and the girls move there. One way and another, we acquired some basic furniture for the house. After a while, Nicky and I fell in love.

Though we were aware that the 28-year age gap would raise eyebrows, we were not going to let that worry us. Nicky's stepmother, Jan, who lived with Nicky's father in Peterborough, was one of the first to see how well-suited we were.

My sisters were equally delighted to hear about the new love in my life. I had remained close to them both, despite the physical distance between us. Veronica had spent most of her adult life in the USA, having moved there at the age of 18 and eventually marrying her boss, Jay Lubkin, and producing 11 children, each one of them brilliant. Veronica taught for some years before realising her dream job as a school librarian. Gabriele had met her husband while she was on a posting to Aden with the RAF. Bernard worked for Mobil oil, a job which took them all over the world before they settled, on his retirement, in Florida, to be near their daughter Pip, her husband David, and their children.

Nicky and I were married in the team church of St Richard's on 31st July 2004 by its vicar, Jonathan Brown. The girls were bridesmaids. Emily was about to turn six and Katie had just celebrated her fourth birthday. It was a joyous occasion. Gabriele and Bernard came from the United States, and Nicky's grandmother, parents and three sisters were there, as well, of course, as my two boys.

My new family moved into the vicarage with me and I became Daddy Francis to Emily and Katie, though they just call me Francis today. I don't remember any problems in suddenly becoming stepfather to two little girls – though perhaps they will remember differently. It's been fun watching them growing up in their different ways: Emily, thoughtful and sensitive like her mother; Katie very active and outgoing.

I wrote to Bishop Lindsay to tell him about my marriage. Diocesan policy was against the remarriage of divorcees, so I wasn't sure how he would react. He sent back a handwritten letter, saying that my news had been a complete – and delightful! – surprise. He even took us out for a pub lunch so that he could meet Nicky. But he also had to tell the Bishop of Chichester, John Hind, whose comment was simply, 'Oh'.

My appointment had been as 'Industrial Chaplain' but I renamed it 'Chaplain to People at Work', which was more accurate. Crawley's industrial estate, Manor Royal, was an obvious place for my ministry. The HR director at Thales, one of the biggest companies on the estate, was very keen to have me. The vetting process took nine months, and by the time it was over, she had left, and her replacement didn't see the need for a chaplain, so that was the end of that. It failed to take off at another factory too. So my chaplaincy ended up being focused in the world of retail. The manager of the County Mall shopping centre, Andrew Bauer, was very enthusiastic, and gave me and my team of volunteers a room to use as a base. Archdeacon William Filby formally opened the new chaplaincy.

We kept a log of where each member of the team had been, so that we covered the mall fairly. It went so well that we started tackling the shopping parades in some of Crawley's neighbourhoods as well.

When the Queen and Prince Philip visited Crawley in 2006, I was invited to meet them in Drucker's Café (now sadly closed). They were first shown round County Mall by Andrew Bauer, where Katie presented Her Majesty with a card and a bouquet. The Queen also met and spoke to Nicky, who was with Katie, Emily and some other pupils from St Andrew's Primary School, where she was then teaching.

The Queen asked me if Gatwick Airport had more employees than Manor Royal – which she had named on a visit in 1950, when she was still Princess Elizabeth. I was able to tell her – thanks to my membership of Gatwick Diamond – that the airport employed 28,000 people, though I did not know the exact number working at Manor Royal, other than that far more people arrived there to work every day than the 13,000 inhabitants of the town who commuted elsewhere. The Queen was very gracious, and left me with a big smile. I remembered how Veronica and I watched the Coronation in 1953, sitting on the floor in the home of a local dentist and colleague of my father, who was the only person we knew who could afford a television set!

After his wife had passed by, Prince Philip asked me, rather naughtily, if there were any Christians living in Crawley! I assured him that there were, and that there were several Christian churches of all denominations in the town, as well as places of worship for the other faith communities.

On my arrival in Crawley I had been appointed the first Senior Chaplain to the Sussex Police by the Chief Constable Paul Whitehouse. I was now chaplain to the Fire Service, too, which sometimes resulted in unusual requests. One day, they said, 'Glad you're here, Francis! We need you to be the passenger in a crashed car.'

Fortunately, I was merely playing the role. The car was on its side and jacked up. They wanted me in the passenger seat, from where they would proceed to lift me out. Getting in was a challenge in itself as I had to climb over the steering wheel. Once in place, I was instructed to act as if I was badly injured. 'Groan, groan,' I muttered, to the amusement of all.

When the Fire Service decided they wanted their chaplains sometimes to wear canvas uniforms, I decided I was too old for that game. It felt the right time to go.

In 2000 I was the only chaplain in the Ambulance Service. One day, when I visited the Sussex HQ in Lewes, I suggested forming a proper chaplaincy – like the police. They said they would discuss this with the unions, whose response was: 'When can you start?' I handed over the police chaplaincy to Ray Smith, then rector of St Wilfrid's, Haywards Heath, in about 2003, and with his blessing, 'poached' some of his chaplains to work a dual ministry. We started with seven in December 2004 and gradually recruited more.

In July 2006, Kent, Surrey and Sussex Ambulance Services merged to become the South East Coast Ambulance Service, and Paul Sutton – the CEO of Sussex – became CEO of the new trust. As Senior Chaplain – a post I held for a further 15 years – I continued to build up our team. At one point we had 26 voluntary part-time chaplains.

It was all very informal back then, even though we wore the green uniform and a green shirt with a clerical collar. If I turned up with a rucksack, they'd say, 'Hi, Francis, are you coming out to play?' which meant, 'Are you coming out on the ambulance for a shift?' Sometimes I'd swap from one ambulance to another at East Surrey Hospital. On one occasion, we had to take a 96-year-old woman to hospital. When her son, who was 74, saw me getting out of the ambulance, he commented that he didn't realise that his mother was so ill that she needed a priest! I had to reassure him that I was there for the crew. On another occasion I assisted the crew by pushing a patient on the ambulance trolley through Sainsbury's, to the surprise of the shoppers who saw us! I really enjoyed working with the Ambulance Service at their HQs – first in Banstead and latterly in Crawley – as well as the Make Ready Centre, where the ambulances are prepared, and on the road.

During the Covid pandemic, chaplains were not permitted to visit stations, although, after shielding for some months because Nicky and I were considered extremely vulnerable for health reasons, I continued my visits to HQ, where I was seen as an essential part of the 'Green Family'. When chaplains' visits to ambulance premises were allowed to resume, some (and in my view totally unnecessary) bureaucracy was introduced, including the requirement that chaplains take various tests on the computer as a condition of continuing their work. I decided it was time to go. At the end of 2021 I retired, leaving the senior role in the safe hands of Paul Fermor, who had been joint Senior Chaplain with me for some time. Sadly, half the team of chaplains also resigned, leaving just 10 of them. I had served as a chaplain, one way or another, for 25 years with the Police, 21 years with the Ambulance Service, and 12 with West Sussex Fire and Rescue Service. I was also chaplain to three Mayors of Crawley during their years in office: Brian Quinn, Bob Burgess and Brenda Burgess.

Despite Bishop John Hind's reaction to my second marriage, he was very supportive when I wrote a sabbatical paper on the Amish in 2006, even providing some money for the project. I first met some Amish people when I was on a road trip with Veronica after an international police chaplains' conference in America. The more I saw and heard about them, the more fascinated I became. I went to Lancaster County in the state of Pennsylvania several times – twice with Nicky and the girls – to see the oldest and largest settlement of the Amish. Not only did I meet some Mennonites there – they are closely related to the Amish, but more liberal – but I also discovered a community of Mennonites living in London.

The Bishop said he'd like to see my paper when it was written.

'I don't agree with your first page,' was one of the first things he said when I went to see him, adding, 'but you like the Amish, don't you?'

Which I admitted I did.

My sister Gabriele died in 2017, sadly predeceased by two of her three children, Michelle and Mark. Bernard continues to live in a retirement complex in Florida.

Veronica was widowed in 2001. She lives in Maryland, although her children are scattered around the USA. We catch up with each other's news every week by video call. It's a ritual we rarely miss.

Billy and his German partner, Angelina, live in Javea on the east coast of Spain with their daughter, Savannah. My ex-wife Greet's health has recently deteriorated, so she is now living in a care home in Javea, a short drive from Billy and Angelina, who are able to visit her and take her out for some meals. Billy is an entrepreneur whose core business is as a supplier of digital TV boxes, but he has fingers in a lot of 'pies'. Ben is a firefighter in Purley, but lives in Pound Hill, Crawley, with his wife Laura. Ben's children Lewis and Lauren are grown up and have left home for university and college respectively. His youngest child, Abbey, who is still at school, now lives with her mother in Kent. Adam, Laura's son from a previous marriage, works in Crawley and has bought a house on a new estate with his long-term girlfriend.

Nicky taught in several primary schools over the years, but decided some time ago to move to a pre-school nursery. While working full-time, she has also been completing an internationally accredited level four diploma in Child and Adolescent Mental Health Coaching, after which she hopes to find a job in that field.

Since January 2023, Nicky has cut her hours at the nursery, so that we can spend more time together, which is really nice! In the early days we enjoyed walking our dogs, especially at Devil's Dyke on the South Downs, Emily and Katie tagging along with us. Hopefully we'll do this again, although walking for me has become more challenging as I approach my 81st birthday.

We have had some special holidays, including to see Veronica in Maryland. (Incidentally, Veronica's partner, Mike, said – and has continued to say – that Emily and Katie were the best-behaved children he had ever known!) We also enjoyed Oslo enormously. Closer to home, we loved Porthcurno, close to Land's End in Cornwall, and Snowdonia, where, among other trips, we travelled on the Ffestiniog Railway and went up Snowdon, also by train – only to find the summit shrouded in fog. Last summer Nicky and I explored the New Forest from the top of buses (!), staying in Milford-on-Sea – a holiday to be repeated! And there have been visits to Nicky's father in Peterborough, and her mother – sadly now in poor health – in Spalding.

During the Covid lockdown, reading and watching TV took over while we were both shielding, although we were also able to spend time in glorious weather in our small garden. Increasing age and a long-term heart condition have limited my activities more recently. But, that said, it is great being married to Nicky, who is such a lovely, caring person and has a heart of gold. I love her to bits!

Nicky has been involved one way or another with Girlguiding for most of her life and has been a leader, including District Commissioner for a while, for 34 years. Emily, too, is a natural with children and has shown a real aptitude for caring for children with special needs. The pair of them run two Rainbow units between them. Both girls attended St Andrew's Primary School followed by the Holy Trinity C of E Secondary School. Emily is a qualified level 3 early years educator. She worked in a local nursery, then left to become a part-time nanny and intern at St John's Church, which was revitalised in 2017 with a new rector, and a team from St Peter's Brighton. That was where she met her boyfriend, fellow intern Alex. In late August 2022, following an extended interview, she was invited to become Kids' and Families' Pastor at the church, a (paid) role that she was delighted to accept. Alex had earlier been appointed Administrator there.

Katie is a qualified Pilates teacher and gym instructor. She and her boyfriend, Oscar, have been together since they were at school. Katie teaches in a variety of places. She spends a few days a week living in Horsham with Oscar and his parents, and teaching Pilates locally; the rest of the time at home. She has just taken on a 30-hour-a-week job at a gym in Crawley. Oscar, meanwhile, recently graduated with a first-class Honours degree, and is now job-hunting.

The past is never far away. I remain in touch with many old friends, colleagues and parishioners. I still speak weekly via Zoom to former students from Downside – one of whom was also at Hemingford Grey with me. David is writing his own account of our schooldays: his memories are quite different from mine – he hated the place!

Nicky and I bought our house from the diocese in 2005, so have no need or desire to move. Although officially 'retired' since December 2012, I remain busy. I am Assistant Priest in the parishes of Crawley and of Worth. I take regular services at St Peter's Church, West Green, and some services, including marriages, at St Barnabas and St Nicholas churches, Worth.

God's train continues to take me on a fascinating ride! I'm in no hurry to get off . . .

An Amish buggy in Pennsylvania

My Long Service Award, as reported on a local website

As Senior Chaplain, November 2013

Firefighter: my son Ben

Ben and Laura

Billy and Ange

Emily

Emily and Alex with Zoe

With my sisters, Gabriele and Veronica, in August 2013

Katie and Oscar at his 2022 graduation

Katie

Nicky with Zoe and Skittles

Royal encounter: Nicky and HM The Queen, on her 2006 visit to Crawley

Dinner near Javea. Left to right: Ben, Savannah, Angelina, Greet, Billy and Laura

Special photo of Nicky

My sister Veronica and her partner Mike

Nicky and me on our wedding day in 2004

Story Terrace

Printed in Great Britain
by Amazon

36380187R00064